Awesome Me!

A Book of Awesome Affirmations for Little Stars!

Cherrie Dejolde Bautista

DEDICATION

This book is lovingly dedicated to my children, Gabrielle and Gizelle, for giving me the inspiration to be the best parent I can be, and to my husband, for unconditionally loving and supporting me, in everything I do.

One special me

is clever and kind,

with a generous heart

and a curious mind.

There's no need to ask

for I know in my heart

I am the most awesome me,

I'm thoughtful and smart!

I can't be held back,

I'm a great bird in flight.

I can reach any goal

I have in my sight.

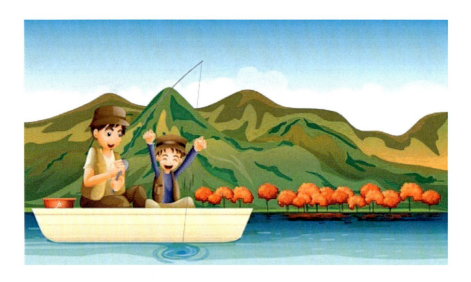

I'm proud of myself,

I've got nothing to hide.

The love that I've got,

it comes from inside.

I'll always be me,

be the best me I can

I'll believe in myself,

be my number one fan!

I am unique,

the most awesome me.

I can be great,

as great as can be!

I know that I'm great,

a big glowing star,

I know if I try

that I can go far.

Although I am small –

one star in the sky,

the light that I bear

can spread far and high.

I love all my friends,

and they love me too.

But before spreading love

You must love You!

I can count on my friends

for support, help, and care,

We believe in each other

anytime, anywhere.

I know that my friends

are all that they seem.

They're helpful and kind

when pursuing my dreams.

I've got lots of great friends,

and the love that we share,

from compassion and goodness,

shows that we truly care.

Within me you'll find

a bright and warm light

made of kind and good deeds,

willpower, and might.

I'm full of joy,

I'm giving and smart.

My light from within

can warm others' hearts.

On this wonder-filled Earth,

I'm just one awesome part,

spreading kindness and cheer

with the light in my heart.

I'm only one light,

but do not ignore

my light is enough

to brighten much more.

I like to have fun,

I run and I play.

I love to live life,

and enjoy every day.

Although I love playing

I like hard work too.

I give my best efforts

in all things I do!

The goodness on Earth

comes from people like me.

It's great to spread love

'cause love is for free.

There isn't a thing

I can't overcome

I believe in myself

to get anything done.

Things can get tough,

but with love, friends, and will

I'll prevail over struggles,

I can climb any hill.

I will climb giant hills,

explore far-off lands

I can do anything

as the person I am.

The person I am

is the most awesome me.

I'm amazing as is,

a big fish in life's sea.

Now that we're through

I know in my heart

I've always been awesome,

an awesome me from the start!

ABOUT THE AUTHOR

Cherrie Dejolde Bautista is a Certified Empowerment Coach committed to help everyone reach their fullest potential and be the best they can be. Having a technical background who worked as an Analyst/Computer Programmer, she pursued and became certified as an Empowerment Coach in her quest to understand how she can become the best parent for her kids.

She realized that in order to raise her kids to be healthy, responsible, confident and successful individuals with a lot of respect for themselves, their family, other people, and life, she needs to empower herself not only to be the best parent, but also to reach her own fullest potential and be the best individual she can be. Being a good role model is the most effective way of teaching, influencing, and nurturing her kids. She teaches her children how to live by letting them watch her do it.

Author's site: http://cherriebautista.com

Author's Other Books

 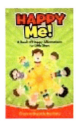 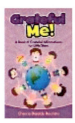  

Thank You!

Your feedback, comments, and suggestions are very much appreciated and valued. Please take the time to post a review at:

http://www.amazon.com/dp/B00BC7OZL0

Your Bonus Gift

To show how much we appreciate you, we are sending you a gift that you and your family can enjoy --- a Free Ebook entitled "**Deliciously Decadent Cheesecake Recipes**" which includes 90 cheesecake recipes that are sure to delight your senses. Now you can easily treat yourself to a delicious homemade slice of heaven or try some of these gourmet cheesecake recipe ideas with friends and family. Please fill out the form at the link below so we can send your Bonus Gift.

http://cherriebautista.com/awesome-me-bonus-ebook/

Made in the USA
San Bernardino, CA
23 March 2016